A View *from* *the* Rough

by **Mike Klemme**

foreword by Tim Hiers

SLEEPING BEAR PRESS
Chelsea • Michigan

Inquiries for reproduction or photography should be directed to:
Golfoto, PO Box 3045, Enid, OK 73702

All inquiries should be addressed to:
Sleeping Bear Press
121 South Main Street
PO Box 20
Chelsea, MI 48118

A View from the Rough
ISBN 0-886947-06-6

Printed in the United States of America
10 9 8 7 6 5 4 3 2 1
Library of Congress CIP Data on File

LIST of COURSES

Governor's Club, Chapel Hill, NC

LIST of COURSES *continued*

FOREWORD

Today, hundreds of thousands of golfers will be lucky enough to be teeing it up for a round of golf. If they take notice, they will also be blessed with a walk through nature to observe God's creations as they live in and around a golf course—creations such as beautiful trees, butterflies, wildflowers, birds, and other wildlife from a cottontail rabbit, to a red fox, or a white-tailed deer. If they didn't already know it, some of the best birdwatching takes place on and around their local golf course.

Like many golfers, the majority of golf course superintendents, myself included, are drawn to the profession not only by the love of the game, but also because of their love of the outdoors and nature. With a few exceptions, they are excellent caretakers and stewards, nurturing the property much like a mother cares for her child or a gardener grows prize-winning roses.

The 1970s ushered in an era of increased awareness of environmental issues. The public began to give close scrutiny to both themselves and to industry in relation to chemical use and maintenance of an ecosystem. With this increased awareness, the golfing industry began to take a long, hard look at issues from design and land use to course management.

Much has changed over the years. The golfing industry, through various allied associations, including the Golf Course Superintendents Association of America (GCSAA) and U.S. Golf Association (USGA), has addressed the public's concerns with integrity, dedication, and education. Its diligent and ongoing research has focused on resource conservation; including energy efficiency, water conservation, habitat and wildlife enhancement, waste management, and reduction in pesticide use through the practical concepts of Integrated Plant Management (IPM).

And still, two major misguided perceptions continue to surface about golf: 1) that golf is an elitist game, made only for the rich; and 2) that it poisons the environment and is detrimental to wildlife. In 1994, seventy-eight percent of all the golf rounds were played on public golf courses and since 1988, over eighty percent of all new golf courses built were public courses. Likewise, research is continuing to show that golf courses, except in rare cases, do not pollute water and can be a true haven for wildlife.

Today, select groups still continue their assault on golf through the media, and even in the school systems, despite the abundance of accurate information to the contrary. Abraham Lincoln once said, "The philosophy in the classroom in one generation will be the philosophy of the government in the next generation." Therefore, it goes without saying that what happens in today's classroom is extremely important.

What have those of us in the profession learned about the critical environmental issues that face golf? We've learned that the truth must be practiced on a daily basis and communicated to the public, many of whom will never set foot on a golf course.

One environmental organization in particular, the Audubon Society of New York State, has chosen to collaborate with golf courses to make them more environmentally friendly. The Society inaugurated the Cooperative Sanctuary Program for Golf Courses with funding and support from the USGA. Their cooperative efforts have increased environmental awareness and improved golf course management, and thereby increased the positive benefits of golf courses.

What about the core concerns of the public, golfer and non-golfer alike? Both share a concern about air quality. They need to know that the average golf course produces enough oxygen to sustain 4,000-7,000 people annually. The sum total of all golf courses in the United States traps an estimated 12 tons of dust and dirt released into the atmosphere by other sources each year. Golf courses help moderate air temperatures in the immediate neighborhood, control soil erosion, serve as a significant fire break and purify—while net recharging—a significant amount of water back into the ground. And, they provide critical habitat for a multitude of diverse species.

Through the outstanding photography of Mike Klemme and captions from an outstanding group of golfers and environmentalists, *A View from the Rough* portrays the diverse efforts of people and institutions dedicated to enhancing the game of golf and the environment. The courses shown are excellent examples of the ability to maintain some of the greatest holes in the world in a fashion that supports and enhances the surroundings.

Golf is an extremely unusual sport in that it transcends, through competition and recreation, all forms of economic and social stratum. It is one of the world's oldest sports, rich in history and tradition. Without compromising its integrity, it addresses the public's concerns and perceptions, and is a key leader in many conservation issues. Golf is truly a major part of the solution, not the problem.

To those who remain sincerely skeptical about golf's good performance and intentions, perhaps the rapidly growing body of evidence that golf courses benefit the environment will satisfy their concerns. But, if they persist in focusing on perceived negatives, in spite of the significant evidence to the contrary, then they should be reminded that sincerity is no substitute for the truth.

I am proud to be part of an industry that takes concern for the environment seriously and like others, will strive to make golf and the environment even better partners in the future. See you on the links.

—**Tim Hiers**

William T. "Tim" Hiers, a Certified Golf Course Superintendent (CGCS), is the Golf Course Manager at Collier's Reserve, Naples, Florida, and was recipient of the 1995 National Environmental Steward Award from the Golf Course Superintendents Association of America. During his tenure, Collier's earned the distinction of becoming the first Audubon Society of New York State Cooperative Sanctuary Signature Golf Course.

INTRODUCTION

Wade Hampton Golf Club

I grew up in a small town in Oklahoma. As a matter of fact, I still choose to live here. All my life I have been surrounded by the beauty of woods, streams and meadows.

Actually, I started my career as a wildlife photographer before moving on to specialize in my other great love—the game of golf.

The differences between the two are not nearly as striking as you might think. For me, it was almost a natural progression. You see, though I have been shooting photographs of golf courses exclusively for the past 12 years, my subjects have hardly changed at all. Confused? Let me try to explain.

I still encounter the same variety of wildlife, the same types of vegetation and the same untamed beauty that I did earlier in my career. The only distinction is that now I am on a golf course, where before, my visits were to national parks, wildlife refuges and botanical gardens.

During this time, I also have seen how golf courses—even in urban settings—can give people an opportunity to escape the hassles of modern living and get back in touch with the natural world. Golf is almost as much a walk in the park as it is a sport.

I hope that by reading this book those of you who love the game of golf and those of you who love God's green earth will come to understand just how much we all have in common.

—**Mike Klemme, 1995**

A View *from* *the* Rough

A pictorial guide to golf and its environment

by **Mike Klemme**

The natural links at Ballybunion, Ireland

It costs no more to follow nature than to ignore her...

—**A.W. Tillinghast**
Golf course architect (1874-1942)

Carmel Valley Ranch, Carmel, CA

Atlantic Golf Club, Bridgehampton, NY

The creation of a golf course can turn an otherwise insignificant tract of land into highly valuable property. The architect's artistic skills and the builder's expertise can transform a desert, an old farm—even an old landfill—into an attractive community asset. The golf course, though, is an exceptional kind of asset, one that requires special management. While an architect and builder may lay the foundation for a truly spectacular golf course, only a professional golf course superintendent can bring it to its full potential.

The professional golf course superintendent serves not only as manager of the golf facility's most valuable asset, but also as the steward of a precious community resource: a living, growing ecosystem. This golf course ecosystem and the larger ecosystem are inextricably linked, just as all types of land uses are linked with a larger ecosystem. In the hands of a professional golf course superintendent, this connection benefits both the environment and the community.

—Stephen F. Mona
CAE, Chief Executive Officer
Golf Course Superintendents Association of America

Industry Hills Resort, City of Industry, CA,
built upon a former landfill

The 15th at Colleton River Plantation, Hilton Head Island, SC

The relationship between a golf course and its environment is one that goes hand-in-hand. The golf course is very much a part of the environment and likewise, the environment is very much a part of the golf course. The two complement each other.

I believe that the surrounding environment helps determine the overall character of the golf course; therefore, the two have to work well together. When I first look at designing a hole, I consider what Mother Nature has already created on that property, and then I try to mold a golf hole that fits very naturally into what is there. I don't believe in forcing an idea on a piece of land, but rather, I blend my ideas with the natural environment and let it help me shape the design of each hole. I guess you could say that Mother Nature is a co-designer of each of my courses.

—**Jack Nicklaus**
Golden Bear International, Inc.

Jasper Park, Jasper, Alberta

On a larger landscape scale, golf courses can be one component of a broader wildlife conservation plan that also includes parks, refuges, and other protected habitats. In this context, the golf course might provide a corridor that connects two or more natural habitats. On the smaller scale, golf courses alone can provide critical habitat for populations of birds, small mammals, reptiles, amphibians, insects and other smaller animals. This dual role makes golf courses an important part of any wildlife conservation planning process.

—**Dr. Peter W. Stangel**
Director
Neotropical Migratory Bird Conservation Initiative,
National Fish and Wildlife Foundation

8

The Boulders Resort & Club, Carefree, AZ

Banff Springs, Banff, Alberta

Spyglass Hill Golf Club, Pebble Beach, CA

The Ocean Course at Kiawah Island, Kiawah Island, SC

Every great golf course appeals to the golfers' senses. While truly enjoying a round of golf, one should be able to smell the flowers and trees, hear the chirping of birds and soft rippling of water, feel the atmosphere, and see the beauty of the way it all comes together for the enjoyment of a natural game that allows us to mingle with nature.

—**Don Cronin**,
Golf Editor
USA TODAY

In urban and suburban environments, golf courses provide significant wildlife habitat. This green space is clearly better than impervious urban surfaces.

—**Dr. James C. Balogh**
Spectrum Research, Inc.
Author, Golf Course Management &
Construction: Environmental Issues

Golf courses provide a great habitat for wildlife, buffer zones to developed areas, stormwater control, green space, noise abatement, dust control, cooling—in short, properly managed golf courses are good for the environment.

—**Dr. Thomas L. Watschke**
The Pennsylvania State University

Pete Dye Golf Club, built on an abandoned coal mine

The scarred hills of north-central West Virginia coal country are today home to one of the country's most visually striking layouts, Pete Dye Golf Club. There are forced carries over flowing brooks, paths that wend across antiquated wooden bridges, a walkway that carries golfers through an actual shaft, a par-5 that lines up with 1,200-foot-high smokestacks in the distance, a sluice that runs out of the side of a green, and a putting surface located under an exposed 65-foot wall formed by the Pittsburgh Seam. Small wonder that golfers are making the trek. There's no better example of how a golf course can enhance the environment. The presumption that golf holes destroy a piece of land has never been more clearly refuted. A scraped-out and abandoned coal field has quickly become one of the game's most distinctive retreats.

—**Dr. Bradley S. Klein**

RESTORING DAMAGED ECOSYSTEMS
with
GOLF COURSES

Pete Dye Golf Club, Bridgeport, WV

Industry Hills Resort, City of Industry, CA

Probably one of the last places most people would choose for a resort location would be a former landfill site in an industrial area of southern California. However, that is just what has been created in the City of Industry. Careful planning has transformed a badly scarred dumpsite into a scenic golf and recreation facility.

In the midst of metropolitan Los Angeles, Industry Hills provides important natural areas, wildlife habitats, and plenty of open space. The 600 acre site includes two 18 hole golf courses, hiking and equestrian trails, and a swim/tennis center, all of which are open to the public. Water conservation is achieved through the use of reclaimed irrigation water, while native and drought tolerant plants are used extensively in the landscape. Methane gas is collected from refuse areas and used as an on-site energy source.

What was once an environmental and economic liability has given way to one of the community's greatest assets.

—Kent Davidson
CGCS, Manager, Golf Courses
Industry Hills Resort, CA

Hilltop Sand & Gravel, Alexandria, VA

Can you visualize this as a golf course? With a great deal of foresight and planning, this eyesore will be converted into a driving range, a practice putting green and, finally, an 18 hole golf course over the next 20 years.

The current owner's father used the land as a chicken farm and then excavated most of the sand and gravel out to be sold commercially; hence the name—Hilltop Sand and Gravel. The gravel pit is now being filled with commercial waste such as wood, concrete, sheetrock, etc. As the pit is being filled, it is being shaped into the contours needed for the future golf course as specified on the grading plans.

The owner estimates that it will take about 20 years to completely fill the site, so the course will be built in three phases, with the third phase being the completion of the 18 hole golf course. Since no trees can be planted on top of the landfill, the design theme will be that of a Scottish highland links type of golf course with lots of mounds and deep bunkers—an amazing transformation for this waste dump.

—**Lindsay Ervin**
Lindsay Ervin & Associates, Inc.

The striking beauty of Black Diamond Ranch, built on an abandoned limestone quarry

Prior to building Black Diamond Ranch golf course, part of the property was land scarred by an active limestone quarry. Its striking beauty is now clearly evident. During the restoration, surface water was redirected to man-made wetlands to filter runoff and protect ground water. Erosion control measures and stormwater management were instrumental in protecting and improving the environment during the construction and in perpetuity.

—Jan Beljan
Design Associate
Fazio Golf Course Designers

The 571 yard, par 5, 18th hole at Spanish Bay Golf Links, Pebble Beach, CA

Spanish Bay may well be the most environmentally sensitive golf course in the world today. After five years of intensive review by the County of Monterey and the California Coastal Commission, approval was successfully obtained to create a golf course that represented the true original character of the property.

What had once been a slightly rolling portion of sandy terrain, we were presented with a parcel of dead flat bedrock where the sand had been mined out years before. Our mission was to restore the property to its original character and feel. We believe we successfully achieved this through the utilization of a large conveyor belt for the importation of sand back onto the property. A careful and detailed shaping process was performed to give the dunes the appearance that they had always been there. Native plant materials were also implemented to add to the natural feeling. This was truly an exercise in recreating linksland. Perhaps the greatest compliment to Spanish Bay is when visitors comment that "the golf course is masterfully laid out amongst the dunes."

—Robert Trent Jones, Jr.
Robert Trent Jones II

SANTA CLARA GOLF CLUB

This former landfill site, located in California's famed Silicon Valley, has been transformed into a popular recreational amenity for the city of Santa Clara. The Santa Clara Golf & Tennis Club handles approximately 100,000 rounds of golf each year and complements the city's adjacent convention center, Westin Hotel, and Great America Theme Park.

The golf course utilizes approximately 150 acres of former landfill. In response to the continuing movement of the landfill, special attention was given to both the drainage and irrigation systems. In addition, turf types and tree species were all carefully chosen to meet the unique environmental characteristics of the landfill.

Drawing upon the skills and creativity of many design and engineering professionals, the Santa Clara Golf & Tennis Club is a fine example of adaptive reuse of the land.

—**Damian Pascuzzo**
Partner
Robert Muir Graves, Ltd.

The Pit Golf Links in Pinehurst, NC, was built on an abandoned sand mine

GOLF COURSES as SANCTUARIES

We let nature influence our entire golf course. We have areas that we let the natural diversity of plants come in, which in turn leads to the diversity of insects, birds, and other wildlife that nature intended.

—**David C. Stone**
Superintendent
The Honors Course, Chattanooga, TN

The Honors Course, site of the
1991 U.S. Amateur Championship

One of the best biological indicators of the ecological health of a golf course is the diversity and number of species of animals found there.

—Dr. James B. Beard
Professor Emeritus
Texas A&M University and International
Sports Turf Institute

The 544 yard, par 5 18th hole at Osprey Point at Kiawah Island

An abundance of wildlife can be found at Robert Trent Jones Golf Club, especially bird life. To date, 104 (and counting) bird species have been inventoried, with at least 48 species nesting on the course. The staff of Robert Trent Jones Golf Club has proved that a top quality playing surface, capable of hosting international tournaments, can be achieved while adhering to ecologically sound management practices.

—Catherine B. Waterhouse
Audubon Cooperative Sanctuary Coordinator
Robert Trent Jones Golf Club, Gainesville, VA

Looking from the championship tee box toward the green on Robert Trent Jones Golf Club's 11th hole. A buffer zone of grasses has been created on the green's hillside to aid in the purification of runoff.

Robert Trent Jones Golf Club Bird Inventory

Common Loon	Broad-winged Hawk	Pileated Woodpecker	American Robin	Rose-breasted Grosbeak
Pie-billed Grebe	Red-tailed Hawk	Eastern Wood-pewee	Gray Catbird	Blue Grosbeak
Horned Grebe	American Kestrel	Eastern Phoebe	Northern Mockingbird	Indigo Bunting
Double-crested Cormorant	Wild Turkey	Great Crested Flycatcher	Brown Thrasher	Rufous-sided Towhee
Great Blue Heron	American Coot	Eastern Kingbird	Cedar Waxwing	Chipping Sparrow
Green-backed Heron	Killdeer	Purple Martin	European Starling	Field Sparrow
Canada Goose	Spotted Sandpiper	Tree Swallow	White-eyed Vireo	Fox Sparrow
Wood Duck	Ring-billed Gull	Barn Swallow	Yellow-throated Vireo	Song Sparrow
Mallard	Mourning Dove	Blue Jay	Warbling Vireo	White-throated Sparrow
Blue-winged Teal	Great Horned Owl	American Crow	Red-eyed Vireo	White-crowned Sparrow
Lesser Scaup	Barred Owl	Carolina Chickadee	Northern Parula	Dark-eyed Junco
Bufflehead	Common Nighthawk	Tufted Titmouse	Yellow Warbler	Red-winged Blackbird
Hooded Merganser	Chimney Swift	White-breasted Nuthatch	Magnolia Warbler	Eastern Meadowlark
Common Merganser	Ruby-throated Hummingbird	Carolina Wren	Yellow-rumped Warbler	Common Grackle
Ruddy Duck	Belted Kingfisher	House Wren	Prairie Warbler	Brown-headed Cowbird
Black Vulture	Red-headed Woodpecker	Golden-crowned Kinglet	Palm Warbler	Orchard Oriole
Turkey Vulture	Red-bellied Woodpecker	Ruby-crowned Kinglet	American Redstart	Northern Oriole
Osprey	Yellow-bellied Sapsucker	Blue-gray Gnatcatcher	Common Yellowthroat	Purple Finch
Bald Eagle	Downy Woodpecker	Eastern Bluebird	Summer Tanager	House Finch
Sharp-shinned Hawk	Hairy Woodpecker	Hermit Thrush	Scarlet Tanager	American Goldfinch
Cooper's Hawk	Northern Flicker	Wood Thrush	Northern Cardinal	

It is important for people to interact with nature. Golf is a sport that encourages interaction with nature. Nature not only accentuates the game, but, in many ways, is the heart of the game. From enduring the elements to navigating your way through the landscapes, the essence of golf is in the pursuit of a unique harmony. This harmony springs from a merger of the mental and physical worlds, striking a sound balance with one's inner voice and eternal challenges.

Recognizing that flirting with hazards can be harmful to one's scorecard is not a difficult realization. In much the same way, tampering unduly with nature can result in damage to the overall ecosystem. The repercussions from such disturbances of nature are not as easily seen as penalty strokes. They can, however, be quite hazardous. For this reason, it is important for people to understand that golf courses hold the potential for good and evil in the face of nature. They can serve to enhance nature and people's accessibility and appreciation for forms of life other than our own. But, it is important to understand that in many cases, excessive chemical applications and inconsiderate land use detract from our natural world and rob species from previously existing ecosystems. Ruthless destruction of existing wildlife habitats or the promulgation of unsustainable development is not an endorsable path for golf courses.

By enacting mission statements that embrace sustainability, adopting integrated pest management strategies, and protecting wildlife habitats, some golf courses are evolving into sanctuaries for nature, and deserve commendation. Links that are striving to achieve these kinds of goals exist and such efforts are to be encouraged. Undeniably, the variety and spice of nature draws many to the game. And remember, when we do not disturb the so-called hazards, they serve to enhance our experience. In being responsible stewards of the Earth, we can ensure a sound future for a game full of honor and respect.

—**Courtney Cuff**
Policy Analyst, Friends of the Earth

The 181 yard, par 3, 12th at Collier's Reserve, Naples, FL

Taking a water sample at Ozaukee Country Club

I urge all superintendents to become involved with the community associations adjacent to their golf course. Volunteer to speak about course operations and the environment at their association meetings; know the officers and board members; volunteer with local environmental groups.

We at Diamond Ridge threw open our shop to *Save Our Streams*, and used the Murphy's Fork Stream, which originates on our back nine, as a teaching laboratory for their members, including a host of teenagers. Here *Save Our Streams* could show their volunteers what a high quality stream looks like and identify those insects that signal a healthy stream, mayflies and stoneflies.

—**George W. Murphy**
Superintendent
Diamond Ridge Golf Course, Woodlawn, MD

Many golf courses today represent a needed green space in a growing community. By being sound stewards of the land, a golf course can become the home of diverse wildlife. Incorporating intelligent plant management with habitat management, a golf course becomes a place to enjoy the game of golf while stimulating a sense of natural beauty.

At Ozaukee Country Club, we take this type of approach. By testing streams, introducing native flowers, creating wildlife food and cover, we have created a beneficial green space for our community while promoting the historic game of golf.

—**Philip M. Bailey**
Naturalist
Ozaukee Country Club

Ozaukee Country Club, Mequon, WI

Semiahmoo Golf and Country Club has long been devoted to environmentally sound turf management practices. In fact, we are currently designated as a Certified Cooperative Sanctuary by the Audubon Society of New York State. This is truly a distinguished honor, and one that we are all very proud of.

Semiahmoo has created over 10 acres of natural grassland and wildflowers adjacent to fairways and tees, and restored the understory of trees and shrubs to their natural state to provide sanctuary for wildlife. Over 300 native trees have also been planted throughout the golf course. As shown in the photo, buffer zones of tall grasses and native aquatic plants were established around ponds to ensure water quality and wildlife habitat.

Continued involvement in protecting and enhancing the environment and wildlife is the responsibility of us all. It is our hope that this philosophy will lead to greater environmental awareness, both locally as well as on the national level.

—**Vance Much**
Superintendent
Semiahmoo Golf & Country Club

Semiahmoo Golf and Country Club, Blaine, WA

Hazeltine National Golf Club, Chaska, MN, site of two U.S. Open Championships

MacKenzie's masterful work with Nature—Cypress Point

WILDLIFE LINKS PROGRAM

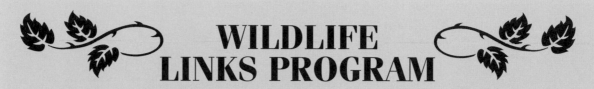

Wildlife Links represents golf's first comprehensive investigation of the game's relationship with wildlife and its habitat. Developed to complement the Audubon Society of New York State's Cooperative Sanctuary Program for Golf Courses, Wildlife Links will assist in funding research on wildlife management issues and will serve as a resource clearinghouse for the golfing industry.

Begun with an initial 3-year $300,000 grant from the USGA, the program will be administered by the National Fish and Wildlife Foundation in Washington, D.C. Dr. Peter Stangel of the Foundation will chair the Wildlife Links advisory board, with other members of the board being Kirk Andries of the International Association of Fish and Wildlife Agencies, Dr. Mike Lennartz of the U.S. Forest Service, Dr. Dan Petit of the U.S. Fish and Wildlife Service, Ron Dodson of the Audubon Society of New York State, Jim Felkel of the U.S. Environmental Protection Agency, and Jim Snow, national director of the USGA Green Section. The advisory committee will be charged with developing a research program to meet the project's goal of protecting and enhancing, through proper planning and management, the wildlife, fish, and plant resources found on golf courses and their native environment.

Dr. Stangel, in describing upcoming activities funded by the Wildlife Links program, said that a primary focus of the group will be the support of credible research in the area of wildlife management, either at universities or on courses themselves. The program will serve as a clearinghouse for information on the subject and eventually will assist in the development of more local resources for golf courses on wildlife enhancement. Plans are underway to develop several management manuals on specific topics such as managing bird habitat on golf courses and protecting and creating healthy wetlands ecosystems. In addition, Dr. Stangel foresees Wildlife Links facilitating local workshops held by wildlife experts for golf course personnel.

Golf courses, especially in more developed regions, hold great potential as hospitable areas for many species of animals and plants. The Wildlife Links Program will provide further knowledge about how golf courses interact with wildlife and the environment.

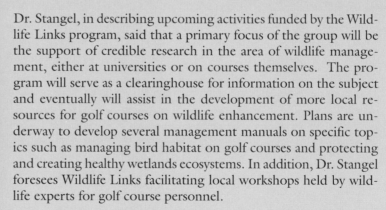

Baltusrol Golf Club, Springfield, NJ, site of several U.S. Open Championships

36

Last night at 5:30, we had a bear on our golf course, the second one in two years. We also have bald eagles, blue herons, hawks, osprey, and even an occasional cougar. We haven't done anything to encourage the wildlife, it is just that the open corridors and responsible management of the golf course are welcomed by these and many more animals.

—Larry Gilhuly
Director, Western Region
U.S. Golf Association-Green Section
commenting on
Canterwood Golf & Country Club
Gig Harbor, WA

Forest Highlands Golf Club,
Flagstaff, AZ

The greatest and fairest things are done by
nature and the lesser by art.

—**Plato**

D'Arcy Ranch Golf Course, Alberta

An eagle surveying his domain at Collier's Reserve

The only bald eagle my 12 year-old son, Nicholas, and I have ever seen in the wild is this one, perched atop his daily observation post near the 17th tee at Collier's Reserve Golf Course, Naples, Florida. We toured the course for a story on the world's first Audubon Society of New York State Cooperative Sanctuary Signature golf course and waited most of the afternoon for the eagle. It was worth the wait. "It's the most magnificent creature I've ever seen," Nick said. I have to agree, and I find it particularly gratifying that this eagle and a mate use a golf course for part of their daily routine. We watched in awe for 15 to 20 minutes, clicking pictures, inching closer as we shot, hoping to get close enough to capture some of the eagle's majesty on film. We were only partly successful, even with a telephoto lens, and settled for near silhouettes and a bit of contrast between the eagle's dark body and magnificent white head. When he'd had enough of our clicking and gawking, the eagle dropped like a stone from the tree and vanished into the marsh grass and scrub pines bordering the course. A few minutes later, we saw him, far away, circling the cloud-flecked evening sky, hunting for his dinner. A magnificent creature indeed!

—Ron Smith
Executive Editor
Southern Turf and Landscape Press

Some of the many residents of Carmel Valley Ranch

We are finding that many well-managed golf courses harbor a greater diversity of wildlife than many parks and refuges.

—Ronald G. Dodson
President
The Audubon Society of New York State

The 473 yard, par 4, 1st hole on the Plantation Course at Kapalua, HI

THE AUDUBON COOPERATIVE SANCTUARY SYSTEM

The largest network of privately owned, cooperatively managed sanctuaries in the world.

The objective of the Audubon Cooperative Sanctuary System (ACSS) is to link various landowners together for the common goals of:

1) creating and enhancing wildlife habitat and
2) conserving and sustaining natural resources.

Members of the ACSS receive information about how to manage their property with wildlife and the environment in mind. Specific programs within the ACSS are:

- Golf Courses
- Schools
- Backyards
- Corporate Properties

Over 1,700 golf, backyard, school, and business properties worldwide are active members.

All members can become Fully Certified Cooperative Sanctuaries by implementing programs in:

- Wildlife and Habitat Management
- Environmental Planning
- Public Involvement
- Water Conservation
- Water Quality Management
- Integrated Pest Management (golf courses)

For more information write to:

Audubon Cooperative Sanctuary System
46 Rarick Road
Selkirk, NY 12158

Hyannisport Club, Hyannis Port, MA

Blue Hills Country Club

Blue Hills Country Club is located on 160 acres in southern Kansas City, Missouri. Like many other golf courses, it is completely surrounded by homes. It is a known fact that people, golfers and nongolfers alike, enjoy being neighbors to a golf course. Why?? It probably has a lot to do with the aesthetics—the outward beauty of a large, green belt situated among the expanses of asphalt, concrete, and wood.

However, many of the homeowners, like those bordering Blue Hills, realize that there is an inward beauty to the course. Beauty reflected in the peacefulness, the greenery, and the wildlife. Blue Hills is a member of the Audubon Cooperative Sanctuary program. We have three large areas set aside as wildlife sanctuaries with bluebird and purple martin houses, bird feeders, and planted in native grasses and wildflowers. Plus, it is not uncommon to see such wildlife as deer, red-tailed hawks, blue egrets, foxes, geese, and once in a while a bobcat wandering on our course. This all sounds like a country setting. However, it isn't; it is situated in a very populated area in south Kansas City. Blue Hills, like many other golf courses, is a tremendous environmental plus to the surrounding community.

—**David W. Fearis**
CGCS, Superintendent
Blue Hills Country Club, Kansas City, MO

The 369 yard, par 4, 9th hole at The Honors Course

World Woods Golf Club, Homosassa Springs, FL

Having played golf for over twenty years and having had the opportunity to visit courses across the U.S. and in other countries, I am surprised that some people are totally unaware of the positive environmental benefits of golf courses. In particular, a golf course can be a sanctuary for a large and diverse group of plants and animals. Throughout the state of Florida, golf course superintendents are taking a very active role in preserving and managing wildlife habitat. This is being done in combination with providing a well-conditioned course for the enjoyment of the golfers.

—John H. Foy
Director, Florida Region
U.S. Golf Association-Green Section

A better understanding of a golf course's diversity, and the necessary integrated management with its surroundings, can enhance the golfer's enjoyment of the game.

—Dr. Kimberly S. Erusha
Director of Education
U.S. Golf Association-Green Section

Ibis Golf & Country Club, Palm Beach Gardens, FL

The best area on the golf course for bird watching is hole #3. The elevated green on this par 3 sits high, with the Cumberland River to the left and wetlands in front and to the right. Behind the green is an 11-acre floodplain woodlot. Because of the contrasting unique habitats of tall grasses, wetlands, woody undergrowth, and dense woodlands all coming together on this hole, the diversity of mammals, reptiles, amphibians, and birds is incredible.

When the acreage that the golf course is on was a farm, approximately 95% of the land was under cultivation. One of our main concerns was to increase the natural habitat on the property. There were only about 20 acres of wildlife habitat; now there are about 80 acres and growing.

—**Shelia M. Finney**
Superintendent
Springhouse Golf Club, Nashville, TN

The demanding 446 yard, par 4, 5th hole at Springhouse

There was some trepidation among golf course architects as new environmental regulations started coming on-line in the mid-1980s. Golf courses have proved remarkably adaptable to advances in environmental thinking and technology. Once the rules were defined, it became quite possible to incorporate wetlands, animal habitat, historical sites and other features into the golf course design, making them more environmentally sensitive.

Golf course architects have always been concerned with preserving the maximum amount of native tree cover and other natural features on the site, so the adaptation was not too difficult. It is appropriate that golf course designers continue to become more environmentally sensitive. One of the key elements of our long-term love affair with the game of golf is the chance to experience natural beauty inherent in well-designed golf courses.

—**Jeffrey D. Brauer**
President
American Society of Golf Course Architects

The 162 yard, par 3, 3rd hole at the Springhouse Golf Club

Initially, I took up the game of golf to gain acceptance and access to diverse and protected habitat areas that may be embraced by courses for birdwatching and wildlife study. Binoculars fit in my golf bag; and I am as critical of how well any course is managed with respect to its ecology and natural aesthetic as the next golfer might be of its greens and playability. For me, the perfect day ends with a decent golf score and a long bird list. Today, my teenage son is a more accomplished golfer and naturalist than I, owing to time we have spent together on the links and in the woods, looking for quail, deer, and my errant golf balls.

—Dr. Jeffrey B. Froke
President
Santa Lucia Conservancy

The 186 yard, par 3, 5th hole at Spyglass Hill

Environmental considerations are highly relevant to the operational management of existing golf courses. A properly maintained golf course requires a much broader approach to management than just turf care. This is important ecologically and also for practical golfing and economic reasons. Furthermore, in accepting the fundamental link between golf and the environment, the golfing world has a duty to strive to preserve and enhance the natural resources with which it is entrusted. This wider awareness is central to the meaning 'Environmental Stewardship'.

It is the goal of the European Golf Association Ecology Unit to develop this golf-environment partnership to the mutual benefit of all concerned. Enhancing the environment and adopting the principles and obligations of Environmental Stewardship means far more than mere minimal compliance with current regulations and health and safety standards. It is a deliberate and proactive decision to share in society's responsibilities to conserve and protect the environment. It should also be the most efficient and cost-effective way of managing golfing facilities and a major contribution to enhancing the golfing experience.

A SUMMARY OF THE ECOLOGICAL ATTRIBUTES OF A GOLF COURSE

CONSERVATION BENEFIT	HOW ACHIEVED
Habitat protection	• Retaining and managing viable habitat units within golf course boundaries. • Ensure adequate space available.
Species protection	• Low disturbance levels in habitat blocks. • Presence of the key habitat requirements. • Specific management policies.
Species diversity	• Range of habitat types; woodland, scrub, hedges, tall and short grassland, wetlands, ditches, streams, ponds.
Habitat links	• Ensure habitat continuity throughout site and adjoining areas. • Ecological basis to design and landscape management. • Partial infilling of habitat gaps in local landscape, facilitating wildlife movement between previously isolated areas.
Buffer zones	• Provision of protected area around sensitive sites. • Limiting spread of urban development into countryside.
Ecotones	• Graduation of habitats. • Sensitive edge management.
Habitat management	• Promote and maintain different successional stages of habitats. • Increase structural diversity of habitats; e.g., different mowing regimes. • Integrated management program for entire golf estate.
Habitat creation	• Ecological basis for planting and seeding program on land of previously low ecological quality.
Scientific research	• Monitoring of habitat creation projects.
Education	• Increase public awareness of ecological relationships of golf.

Reference: *An Environmental Strategy for Golf in Europe*, European Golf Association Ecology Unit, 1995.

For additional information, contact the European Golf Association Ecology Unit at Chaussee de la Hulpe 110, B-1050 Bruxelles, Belgium.

Royal Birkdale Golf Club, site of Arnold Palmer's stunning Open Championship victory in 1961 and host to the 1997 Open Championship

Cranberry Resort is located on Georgian Bay in the town of Collingwood. The resort's owner and operator, Law Development Corporation has empowered the staff at Cranberry to pursue environmental excellence. The decision was made to join the Audubon Cooperative Sanctuary Program for Golf Courses, and in less than a year the golf course was granted complete certification. The work does not end here, initiatives are constantly being undertaken to improve Cranberry's Environmental Management Plan. One of the ongoing initiatives is to educate golfing and nongolfing public to the fact that golf courses and the environment are not two polar extremes and that they can coexist.

—**Greg Williams**
Superintendent of Golf & Grounds Maintenance
Cranberry Resort, Collingwood, Ontario

Mini-sanctuaries such as the one pictured are located throughout the Cranberry Resort Golf Course. Here Purple Martins and bats assist with the integrated pest management program.

All plantings within and around Cranberry Resort Golf Course must have wildlife food value. Cranberry tries to use as many native perennials as possible; however, when annuals are used, they must also meet the food value requirements, and be noninvasive.

Native plants provide the golfer with year-round color, and the wildlife with food. Buffer zones around ponds help in maintaining water quality and provide cover for wildlife.

Wetlands act as natural sponges, holding spring runoff and slowly releasing the water to the course throughout the summer, thus reducing the need for irrigation. Such areas also provide wildlife with travel corridors.

Ecologist Scott Martin, of Wild Canada, works closely with the Cranberry Resort superintendent and staff to ensure that projects are run in an ecologically sound manner, and that this information is communicated to the public through a series of nature hikes and programs conducted on golf course property.

The windblown links at Crowbush Cove, Morell, Prince Edward Island

In many cases, golf courses may provide the last remnant of habitat in an urban environment. With thoughtful planning and management, golf courses can be good habitat for wildlife, from birds to butterflies to fish. Wildlife on golf courses enhances the golfing experience, and golf course habitats can play an important role in local and regional wildlife conservation plans. Programs such as the U.S. Golf Association's Wildlife Links are designed specifically to help golf course managers achieve these twin objectives.

—**Dr. Peter W. Stangel**
Director, Neotropical Migratory Bird
Conservation Initiative
National Fish and Wildlife Foundation

Golf courses can act as an effective buffer between rural or wilderness areas and urban sprawl.

—**Teri Yamada**
National Director
Royal Canadian Golf Association-
Green Section

Glen Abbey Golf Club, Oakville, Ontario, site of the Canadian Open

Queenstown Harbor Golf Links, Queenstown, MD

If land is to be developed, only golf courses end up
providing at least 150 acres of open space, wetlands,
forests, and other habitats, making golf one of the
best forms of sustainable development.

—Ronald G. Dodson
President
The Audubon Society of New York State

Course architect, Lindsey Ervin, standing in one of the naturalized areas on the Queenstown.

Conversion of the Queenstown property from its previous agricultural use to a golf course has resulted in significant documented improvement to the water quality and wildlife habitat of the surrounding area.

County regulations expanded the 25 foot agricultural setback from tidal waters of the Chesapeake Bay to 300 feet, and design criteria established topographical contouring that directs all runoff into 11 excavated ponds that double as features for the course. Additionally, an Integrated Pest Management (IPM) program is fully implemented and results in minimal use of chemicals on the course.

Since the completion of the course, 15 ground water monitoring wells located throughout the project have demonstrated a methodical decrease in nitrate-nitrogen levels in the water. The most recent monitoring in March, 1995, contained an average of 3.0 milligrams per liter—70% below the drinking water standard. This translated to direct reductions of nitrogen inputs to the saline waters of Little Queenstown Creek, the Chester River, and Chesapeake Bay.

Queenstown Harbor has also worked closely with local conservation groups such as Chesapeake Wildlife Heritage and Horsehead Wildlife Sanctuary to enhance wildlife habitat and establish wetland and wildlife educational programs for regional elementary schools.

Today, it is impossible to play the course without glimpsing the many residents of the area—deer, fox, squirrels, muskrats, bald eagles and countless shore birds—herons, geese, swans, and ducks. When play is done and day darkens into night, Queenstown reverts to the natural world it has always been a part of, once again.

—Lex Birney
Owner
Queenstown Harbor Golf Links

With Queenstown Harbor's blessing, Chesapeake Wildlife Heritage has installed wood duck nest boxes in the marshland surrounding the course. These nest boxes have been responsible for boosting the wood duck population in the area.

—Ned Gerber
Chesapeake Wildlife Heritage

Atlantic Golf Club, Bridgehampton, NY

Every property that will be developed into a golf course presents its own special problems and challenges. As the architect on the project, we are charged with addressing each issue in an environmentally conscious fashion while constructing a course that will be both beautiful and challenging.

At the Atlantic Golf Club in Bridgehampton, New York, in addition to the normal concerns in course construction, we were faced with the existence of two endangered species on the property, the northern harrier hawk and the eastern tiger salamander. We worked with the Group for the South Fork and The Nature Conservancy to develop appropriate measures for dealing with the additional challenge presented by endangered species. Several design features were employed, including revegetating wetland areas through reintroduction of native Long Island grasses and shrubs that had been lost in decades of farming the property.

By utilizing the high ground for golf and enhancing the slopes to wetlands, we have created a golf course which is truly visually exciting. The course will play differently each day due to the varying conditions of the wind. It is the type of golf course that one can continually enjoy, and it is a true example of a course designed in harmony with nature.

—Rees Jones
Rees Jones, Inc.

In the game of golf the rough is a place to be avoided. The penalty for wandering into the rough zone is lost balls and added strokes. A golf course with truly intimidating rough is one that appears to have been dropped into the natural surroundings. Birds squawk, crickets chirp, alligators grumble, squirrels chatter, and frogs croak in a symphony that welcomes the golfer to spend a few hours wandering around their home. For me, golfing in a park is far more pleasurable than golfing in a pasture.

—**Steve Beeman**
President
Ecoshores, Inc.

Collier's Reserve

The application of appropriate agricultural chemicals for proper presentation and preservation of our nation's golf courses poses no threat whatsoever to the adjacent ground water supplies when those chemicals are properly stored, handled, and applied; and thus no public health impact.

—**Dr. Jay Lehr**
Executive Director
National Ground Water Association 1967-1991

SOME FACTS ON GOLF

Oakmont Country Club, site of Ernie Els' 1994 U.S. Open Championship victory

THE ROLE OF TURFGRASS
IN ENVIRONMENTAL PROTECTION

1. Turfgrass reduces loss of topsoil from wind and water erosion.

2. Turfgrass absorbs and filters rain and runoff water, recharging ground
    and surface water.

3. Turfgrass captures and cleans runoff water from urban areas.

4. Turfgrass improves the soil and restores damaged areas
    (e.g., landfills, mining sites).

5. Turfgrass improves air quality and moderates temperature.

6. Turfgrass reduces noise, glare, and visual pollution.

7. Golf course turfgrasses, trees, shrubs and water features create
    and enhance wildlife habitats.

8. Turfgrass and golf enhance physical health.

9. Golf contributes to the community's economy.

Reference: *Journal of Environmental Quality*, Volume 23, #3, May/June 1994.

The Audubon Society of New York State's Cooperative Sanctuary Program for Golf Courses, initiated under the sponsorship of the U.S. Golf Association, has led to changes in management of golf courses that have benefitted wildlife and reduced pesticide use and risk on a number of courses. Over 1,500 courses have now signed onto this program and are working toward certification, and a number have already earned this distinction.

—**Anne R. Leslie**
Chemist
U.S. Environmental Protection Agency

Turfgrass is God's natural carpet. What is most amazing is that it is also His natural filter and purifier.

—**Dean L. Knuth**
Senior Director
U.S. Golf Association-Green Section

In the majority of water samples taken from properly managed golf courses, there have been no detectable levels of pesticides, and if they have been detected, the levels are below drinking water standards.

—**Dr. Thomas L. Watschke**
The Pennsylvania State University

Ground water contamination is a growing problem, with over 10,000 documented cases nationwide. Yet the cost of removing contaminants is so high that it is often cheaper to attempt to develop a new water supply than to clean up an existing one. At the same time, the need for clean, potable water is increasing. In the last decade, the U.S. population rose by 20 million, while the amount of ground water available for consumption (about 15 quadrillion gallons) remained the same.

Recent efforts to identify sources of ground water contamination have uncovered many culprits. But the common ingredient in every incident is mankind's use and abuse of the land and its subsurface. Golf courses, in particular, have been unfairly singled out in the debate over protecting ground water and coastal water resources. Properly designed and managed golf courses can provide tremendous protection of ground water systems-protection that far surpasses that available if the land were developed, and is second only to allowing the land to remain in a natural state for conservation purposes.

—**Jon D. Witten**
President
Horsley & Witten, Inc.

When the subject of golf courses and the environment arises, a picture of Pebble Beach Golf Links and the Links at Spanish Bay frequently appears in my mind. The first time I looked down on the 7th green at Pebble Beach, there were seashore grass roughs around me, I saw and heard waves crashing below, a clean sea breeze was blowing, and sea gulls were flying gracefully. It took my breath away. It was the kind of feeling I have experienced rarely in only a handful of other places around the world. This feeling was enhanced by the knowledge that these two nearby courses have been truly integrated into the wildlife, plant, and physical environments. In the case of Spanish Bay, there was even an improvement of the environment, a restoration to what had existed before sand mining took its toll.

But appearances don't tell the whole story about how golf courses may or may not impact the environment. Scientists much prefer data over pretty pictures. Fortunately, there is a growing set of surface water and ground water quality monitoring data on pesticide and fertilizer impacts. The first important study in this area monitored ground water at four golf courses on Cape Cod in the mid to late 1980s. Since then, we have reviewed monitoring data from 13 studies of 25 golf courses from Massachusetts to Guam. What do we conclude? *Water quality impacts by golf turf management are minimal and usually nonexistent.* State-of-the-art integrated pest management techniques should be used so that pesticides are only applied when necessary. Golf courses and the environment can and do coexist.

—Dr. Stuart Z. Cohen
CGWP, President
Environmental & Turf Services, Inc.

Water quality impacts by golf turf management are minimal and usually nonexistent.

The deceptive 7th at Pebble Beach

GOLF COURSES
AS
ENVIRONMENTAL STEWARDS

It is time for golfers to understand that modern management practices allow our golf courses to live in harmony with nature. Golf course superintendents should be proud of the fact that we have successfully implemented Integrated Pest Management programs that follow sound cultural practices and reduce the use of chemicals. It takes a great deal of skill, technical knowledge, and environmental expertise to keep up with the ever-increasing demands for higher quality playing surfaces.

Professional golf course superintendents are true environmentalists. As caretakers of the land, we give top priority to selecting maintenance practices that are safe for the environment. Today's golf course superintendents are aware of and care about the consequences of overuse of pesticides and fertilizers. There is not a more environmentally aware and sensitive group than today's golf course superintendents.

—**Gary T. Grigg**
CGCS, President
Golf Course Superintendents Association of America

Forest Highlands, Flagstaff, AZ

The Resort at Squaw Creek, built on top of an aquifer, has been devoted to keeping environmental issues its primary concern. Constant monitoring of ground water, surface water, and wetlands has shown the Resort to be a big asset to the Lake Tahoe area. Squaw Creek has been able to maintain high quality conditions even with a no pesticides and a low fertility program.

—**Michael Carlson**
Superintendent
Resort at Squaw Creek

The pristine environment at Squaw Creek, Olympic Valley, CA

The 10th at National Golf Links, Southampton, NY, one of many awe-inspiring views and great golf holes

We can reduce turfgrass disease and thus the need for chemicals on our golf courses with proper management techniques. Through careful observation, Integrated Pest Management, and appropriate maintenance procedures it is possible to have a beautiful and naturally presented golf course which fits in with the surrounding environment.

—Karl E. Olson
CGCS, Superintendent
National Golf Links of America

One of the most subjective issues concerning the environment and golf is probably never more apparent than in my home state of Arizona. Our state has done a marvelous job concerning water conservation and preservation of its existing arroyos and surroundings. Because the practice of irrigating a limited amount of turf is enthusiastically accepted by the vast majority of golfers, shouldn't this then be a consideration for any golf course anywhere in the world?

—**Tom Weiskopf**
Tom Weiskopf Signature Designs

Today's golf course irrigation systems should more appropriately be called "*water management & conservation systems.*" By combining the speed and timing accuracy of computers connected to environmental sensors and weather stations, with sprinklers that distribute water more uniformly, these water management systems can automatically apportion water precisely to the varying needs of the plants. In addition to computer controlled irrigation systems for golf courses, more naturalized areas, reused wastewater for irrigation, and grasses that require less water give superintendents the resources to keep a finely-tuned, ecologically healthy golf course.

—Rod McWhirter
National Specifications Manager
Rain Bird-Golf Division

Desert Highlands, Scottsdale, AZ

I wish all people who think golf courses are bad for the environment could walk around Troon just before dusk and see the rabbits, quail, and other animals by the hundreds feed along the edge of the fairway.

—Jay Morrish
Jay Morrish & Associates, Ltd.

Troon Golf & Country Club, Scottsdale, AZ

Environmentally sensitive development is not only possible but in the best interest of all communities. A properly designed, landscaped, and managed golf course can be a tremendous asset to any community-both economically and environmentally.

Our efforts today are concentrated on maximizing the efficiency with which we utilize natural resources. Recent implementation of state-of-the-art irrigation software and turf-specific irrigation equipment will benefit both our golf course operation and, as a result, the High Sonoran Desert environment.

—Paul K. Skelton
CCM, Vice President/General Manager
Troon Golf & Country Club

The natural beauty of Sand Hills Club, Mullen, NE

The 183 yard, par 3, 9th hole on the Bluegrass Course at Old Westbury Golf & Country Club, Old Westbury, NY

As one component of their environmental management plan, Old Westbury Golf & Country Club has developed a composting plan. Club superintendent Phil Anderson initiated the program that utilizes organic debris generated on the site as well as through a cooperative program with the Village of Old Westbury. Through this mutually beneficial arrangement, the Village disposes of yard waste and the Course produces rich composted soil. By the spring of 1995, Anderson had composted between 8,000 and 10,000 yards of debris, of which 75 percent was generated by the Village.

OLD WESTBURY GOLF & COUNTRY CLUB
CODE OF ENVIRONMENTAL CONDUCT

PREAMBLE

The game of golf is enhanced by and is, indeed, dependent upon the natural surroundings. The quality of golf and life is enhanced by the conservation of our natural resources. The Club is committed to take every practical precaution toward ensuring that the products and techniques used in the maintenance of the golf course present the lowest possible risk to the environment or to the health and well-being of members, employees, guests, and neighbors.

A properly maintained golf course, with established turfgrass cover and mature tree stands, provides much-needed greenspace relief from urban development. The filtering ability of dense, healthy turf and its thatch layer can be utilized to ensure pollutants do not reach ground water or run off to streams. The golf course provides for the preservation or creation of areas useful to wildlife. When managed in an environmentally conscious manner, the golf course enhances the quality of life for its members and the community.

The goal is to develop programs and execute practices that sustain an equilibrium between maintaining quality playing conditions and a healthy environment. The Club acknowledges the need to blend governmental regulations with self-initiated plans to achieve and maintain this balance. It also recognizes that all regulations and plans should be based upon scientifically supported data and to this end, will continue to support turfgrass research.

Golfers can help to provide the highest quality experience and preserve the same natural experience for future generations by supporting the Club's efforts to balance conditioning with environmental enhancement and conservation strategies.

Barton Creek Club, Austin, TX

A naturally occurring limestone-lined water feature behind the first green on the Barton Creek Fazio Course is enhanced by recirculating a combination of stormwater and spring water with electric motors. These recirculated water features also serve to cleanse stormwater runoff by trapping sediments, while aquatic plants utilize and remove nutrients. By irrigating this cleansed water back onto the golf course, Barton Creek is effectively recycling the water and cleaning it twice through nature's own filters—wetlands, vegetation and soil.

On this 10th hole, native plant materials were salvaged from future roadways and fairways, and replanted adjacent to boulevards and throughout the golf courses to help maintain the natural environment and minimize the need for irrigation and pest controls. The cliff in the background lines the edge of our course's namesake, Barton Creek.

—Timothy D. Long
President
Barton Creek Landscape, Inc.

The entire Audubon Sanctuary Program for Golf Courses has provided a communication vehicle that has long been needed in the golf industry. This program has allowed many of us in the industry, who have for years approached the overall management of the properties in a very environmentally responsible manner, to document and improve ongoing strategies. Programs were developed that have allowed all involved to develop a new awareness that human use can, in fact, coexist and enhance the ecologies of the properties. This program has become a center point of our intern program that in turn produced our fine certification report and began a large variety of intern opportunities that can range from agronomy through the environmental sciences.

There will always be naysayers, but the fact stands that this flow of educational awareness doesn't stop with the students and staff. It includes our members, local secondary school students that may be brought in to participate, and even the community will benefit from the preservation of this open space known as the Hyannisport Club.

—**Charles T. Passios**
CGCS, Golf Course Manager
Hyannisport Club

Hyannisport Club, Hyannis Port, MA

A special project that has been very successful at Hyannisport Club is the raising of a large platform to attract osprey. The osprey platform is in an area of the course that is restricted from human interference. The platform is clearly visible on the golf course, but is far enough away to avoid human pressures. This past summer, four young osprey were fledged. The osprey use the entire golf course for their feeding ground and can be spotted at the pond, the salt marsh, over the woodlots, or near the creeks, hunting for food.

Whistler Golf Resort, Whistler Village, British Columbia

Golf's greenkeepers—golf course superintendents—have sometimes been forced to defend their practices concerning the environment. A study in Canada, for example, showed that between 1989 and 1993 there was a 60% decrease in the amount of money spent annually on both herbicides and insecticides. These "medicines" for turf are usually at the centre of opponents' arguments saying that golf courses use them indiscriminately. In fact, because of efficient, effective, and intelligent use of land and concern for nature, many golf courses thrive in locations deemed unsuitable for other uses.

If it weren't for golf courses, cemeteries, and the occasional urban park, many of North America's urban centres would be paved over. Golf superintendents are true environmentalists—they work day in and day out preserving, protecting, and enhancing the environment for which they are responsible.

—**R. Vince Gillis**
Executive Director
Canadian Golf Superintendents Association
Association Canadienne Des Surintendants De Golf

People need to realize that golf course superintendents are also members of the community and that they and their families are part of all environmental impacts from golf courses. Because of their education and awareness to these issues, these "stewards of the land" are our strongest advocates. It is to our advantage to have them in these important positions.

Turfgrass science and management is a small, but increasing part of agricultural sciences. What sets turfgrass apart from the rest of agriculture is that turfgrass is measured by quality, not yield. While yield is normally achieved by increasing inputs such as water, fertilizers, and pesticides, turfgrass quality is maximized by using these inputs in very precise, judicious amounts. Golf course superintendents have long recognized this strategy, and their efforts are continually geared in these directions.

—**Dr. John N. Rogers, III**
Michigan State University

I consider myself to be an environmentalist. At the Oregon Golf Club, we go to extremes to make sure we use pesticides and fertilizers in the safest and minimalist way possible. Superintendents today receive a wealth of information on what pesticides to use and how to use them. Combined with common sense, this knowledge enables the environmentally proper management of the golf course.

The Oregon Golf Club, in partnership with the Oregon State Parks, is putting in a nature trail through the golf course to the state park which, with the golf course, will also serve as a wildlife corridor.

—**John Anderson**
Superintendent
Oregon Golf Club

The 18th at Shinnecock Hills, site of Corey Pavin's clutch 4-wood shot to win the 1995 U.S. Open Championship

I have a belief that not only can a golf course and the environment exist together, but that the golf course should be one of its most valued assets.

Over the past six years, the Robert Trent Jones Golf Club has proved that it can be a responsible neighbor. The course, built on the shores of a drinking water reservoir in Lake Manassas, was designed with an extensive water retention system installed, and the quality of the drinking water has actually improved over this period. We have instituted a sound IPM program which emphasizes efficient use of fertilizers and pesticides, and most importantly—WATER. I am very proud of our accomplishments to date and our work with the Audubon Cooperative Sanctuary Program for Golf Courses.

—Glenn Smickley
CGCS, Superintendent
Robert Trent Jones Golf Club, Gainesville, VA

In recent years at Franklin Hills Country Club, forty-five acres of nature-sensitive area have been created within this suburban setting. Among this acreage are included two natural ponds and a wetlands, home to wood ducks, mallards, kingfishers, and great blue herons. The forested and heather areas of the property provide homes and food for white tail deer, red fox, red-tail hawk, possum, raccoon, skunk, woodchuck, and rabbit. The club has been a member of the Audubon Society of New York State Cooperative Sanctuary Program since 1992, and has installed over 75 nesting boxes that attract over 15 additional varieties of birds.

—Tom Gray
CGCS, Superintendent
Franklin Hills Country Club, Franklin, MI

The protected site at Loch Lomond

It has been said that Loch Lomond Golf Club in Scotland rests on a site most architects would sell their souls for. Given its profound beauty, we enjoyed one of our biggest successes in protecting the environment at Loch Lomond. One of the largest issues on the site was the trees, many of which are over 300 years old. Some are more than 600 years old.

We gave tremendous respect to this in the routing, which goes alongside Loch Lomond, through the pine forests, along wetlands and past redwoods, yews and oaks. A very specialized drainage system was installed which protected a beautiful copper beech. The potential issue of erosion along the Loch shore was addressed and there is now an increase in wildlife on the property, with more hawks, herons, songbirds, oyster catchers, Canadian geese, and an abundance of pheasants and deer.

Loch Lomond is a protected site. We are pleased to have been given this extraordinary opportunity to work within a remarkable setting.

—**Tom Weiskopf**
Tom Weiskopf Signature Designs

Shoreacres Club, Lake Bluff, IL

Ravines bisect or parallel 14 of the 18 holes at Shoreacres. While some of the ravines are maintained as playable turf, many are naturalized like the 14th hole above. These naturalized settings afford abundant habitat for many plant and animal species.

In a cooperative effort with county environmentalists, we attempted to expand the northshore bluebird flyway by mounting bluebird boxes in several locations on the course. Our efforts have been rewarded, having fledged from 20-40 young each year. In addition, a red-tailed hawk has taken up residence at Shoreacres and produced 1-2 young each of the last six years.

The membership enjoys sharing their golf course with the wildlife who have made Shoreacres their home.

—Timothy F. Davis
Superintendent
Shoreacres Club, Lake Bluff, IL

Devil's Paintbrush, Caledon, Ontario

A great golf course doesn't simply fit into the environment, it *is* the environment. It is nonsense to separate a golf course from its surroundings because one is maintained. In fact, it may be because golfing ground is managed, that makes it an ever better "environment" than the unmanaged areas that surround it. Despite being a landscape whose visual qualities soothe and relax the human spirit, a golf course supports a web of life as complex as any untouched wilderness. Building a golf course rarely displaces indigenous plants and animals, and in fact expands the biodiversity of the site. Quietly observe a golf course, over the entire day and night, and you, too, will realize that a golf course is a complete environment.

—**Dr. Michael J. Hurdzan**
Hurdzan Golf Course Design

Arrowhead Golf Club, Littleton, CO

Elk River Country Club, Banner Elk, NC

Golf as a recreational activity and the maintenance of the course developed not aside from, but as a part of, nature. In any golf course situation, the playability of the course is dependent upon the design **and** the maintenance. After the design blends the desired effects of the playing of the game into the natural environment, it is the responsibility of the golf course superintendent to maintain that integrity of the course with natural surroundings.

While today's golfer insists on more exacting playing conditions than his predecessors, this need not be at any environmental expense. A well conditioned course still primarily depends on the basic cultural practices of proper mowing, fertilization, and irrigation, in that order, for the maintenance of the playing conditions. The golf course superintendent has the responsibility for ensuring that these practices are implemented in a timely manner, something that has not changed over the centuries. What is different today is that the superintendent is better educated, has access to more information on which to make decisions, has more resources available for course maintenance, and has a better understanding of their responsibility as a steward of the environment.

—**Dr. Charles H. Peacock**
North Carolina State University

Sawgrass Country Club

I spend a good deal of time in the inner cities. Many of the playgrounds have been paved over. The turf that remains is seldom irrigated, goes dormant and turns brown in the warm dry weather of summer. Then, suddenly, there is a golf course with its green grass and the wind gently blowing the leaves on the trees that line the fairways. All of a sudden you feel a little cooler, and even mentally refreshed, by the sight of the green grass. In many places, golf courses are the only green space left in the inner cities and without them they would be even more unbearable places to live.

We have learned so much about how to maintain healthy turf on golf courses while reducing the use of persistent pesticides. This has been accomplished through little things like irrigating during the day instead of at night to reduce disease problems. Daily irrigation has also raised the threshold level for insecticides applications for grub control. In addition, it has eliminated the need for insecticides to control chinch bugs and billbugs. The use of organic fertilizers has greatly reduced the need for fungicides to control turfgrass diseases. Computer prediction models are being used to determine when fungicide applications should be made. By using these computer models, fungicide applications are made only when the environmental conditions are present for a particular turfgrass disease to occur instead of applying them every two weeks all season long for fear that a disease might occur. With some of the new biological controls of diseases, insects, and weeds in the pipeline, I believe we will continue to see fewer and fewer pesticides used on golf courses in future years and more reliance on alternative pest control measures.

we will continue to see fewer and fewer pesticides used on golf courses

—Dr. Joseph M. Vargas, Jr.
Michigan State University

Maidstone Club, East Hampton, NY

THE NATURE OF GOLF

It's almost unfair. Not only does Michigan have 36,000 miles of rivers and streams and 11,000 inland lakes that create endless recreational opportunities for residents and visitors, we're also the home of 720 public golf courses—more than any other state in the nation. Anywhere you go in our Upper or Lower Peninsulas, you can swing the clubs—even on historic Mackinac Island.

Golf in the Great Lakes State, wherever it is played, is a celebration of nature. Our courses merge trees, land, water, and sky into colorful portraits that are remembered long after the round is complete. The serenity found on our tees, fairways, and greens provides a welcome escape to anyone caught in the rapid pace of life.

A sport for all ages, golf draws people to Michigan from across the Midwest and beyond. Its impact on our economy is anything but minimal. I know this because when I play golf, I am a major contributor to our economy. Golf balls aren't cheap.

—**Governor John Engler**

Garland Resort, Lewiston, MI

The difficult 185 yard, par 3, 10th hole

Imagine being on hand for every sunrise at the world's most beautiful property, and you can easily understand a superintendent's enthusiasm for and appreciation of the successful marriage between golf and nature. Conservation and environmental enhancement are natural offspring of this rapport superintendents have with the earth.

—P. Stan George
CGCS, Superintendent
Prairie Dunes

P.J. Boatwright's favorite par 5, the 17th at Prairie Dunes, Hutchinson, KS

The 161 yard, par 3, 2nd hole at Prairie Dunes with its tough 2-tier green

Golf and nature can coexist to a much larger extent if a greater number of courses follow the lead of habitat protection, ecological integrity, and minimal disturbance. The large amount of natural habitat on these courses not only makes for exciting golf, but also supports wildlife, prevents water runoff, reduces irrigation, and decreases chemical inputs.

—Dr. Max R. Terman
Tabor College

Lahinch Golf Club, Ireland

A golf course that consisted entirely of one shade of green would be merely ugly. There is great charm and beauty in the varying shades of colour of a golf course.

—Dr. Alister MacKenzie
Golf Course Architect
(1870-1934)

The striking design at High Pointe Golf Club, Traverse City, MI

I firmly believe that we can build environmentally friendly courses, without needing to create incredibly complicated, man-made ecosystems to "handle" the chemicals. High Pointe, my first solo design, takes the same approach as the golf courses I saw during my year in the British Isles: we experimented with fescue grasses on the fairways and greens to minimize pesticide use on the sandy soil. The low maintenance turf rewards good play: approaches to the greens are left open in front but carefully contoured, so players still have a chance to find the green from a less-than-perfect lie. The golfers appreciate the lower green fees which come from a lower maintenance budget; the developer appreciates the fact that it's still the same beautiful piece of land it was when we started.

Alister MacKenzie aspired to build courses which provided "the greatest good for the greatest number"—not just for the average golfer, but even for the average citizen. The **more we respect** the landscape in building our courses, the more people will become exposed to the attractions of golf and the environment.

—**Tom Doak**
President
Renaissance Golf Design

During my fifteen years as a golf course superintendent, my job responsibilities have grown to include as much public relations, government regulations, and environmental issues as agronomics. As manager of Boone Links and Lassing Pointe Public Golf Courses in Kentucky and an avid outdoorsman, amateur environmentalist, and father of three boys, I've sometimes wrestled with the proper balance between my job as superintendent and as steward of the environment. Through the Audubon Cooperative Sanctuary Program, I found the perfect way to successfully combine these roles.

As part of the "public involvement" aspect of our Cooperative Sanctuary, Boone County's environmental committee placed a particular emphasis on nature education programs with local school groups. To get started, I decided to invite my wife's junior high school science class for an educational tour of the golf course.

On the appointed day, 70 enthusiastic sixth graders arrived, eager to see the course and learn about how we manage it as a sanctuary. They were totally amazed that a family of red-tailed hawks had recently fledged three chicks right smack in the middle of our course. Finding animal tracks, dens, and food sources really excited their imaginations.

Lassing Pointe Golf Club

After a two-hour tour of the grounds, the students participated in a question and answer session over hot chocolate and snacks. The students then wrote essays on the habitat and environment they observed at the course. I shared the essays with my staff and the results were extremely satisfying and a big morale booster. The crew seemed especially pleased that the kids had shown such an interest in our recent GCSAA Environmental Stewardship Award. A few even asked how they could get such a neat job.

As a result of our tour, many students who would never have had the opportunity to visit a golf course, now have a positive outlook and perception of the game of golf and its environment. They know more about the wildlife and habitats that thrive on our course and are better educated about our efforts to responsibly manage this environment.

Plans are now underway for inviting more schools to visit Lassing Pointe Golf Course. I'm already excited about this season's crop of new pupils.

—**Jerry Coldiron**
CGCS, Superintendent
Lassing Pointe and Boone Links Golf
Courses, KY

Osprey Point at Kiawah Island uses recycled wastewater for its irrigation of the golf course, none of which reaches the pristine freshwater marshes and wetlands. The course is also home to many species of wildlife, and supports many families of bobcats in its surrounding natural areas.

—**Steve Miller**
Superintendent
Osprey Point Course at Kiawah Island, SC

A golf course couldn't exist without the natural environment—they are eternally intertwined. Part of being a good golf course superintendent is to always think of the big picture, not just of 18 greens, tees, and fairways. Our mandate is to provide the best playing conditions possible in an environmentally thoughtful way. Education, past experience, and common sense all contribute to this very achievable goal. We, as golf course superintendents, owe much to the natural environment—it not only provides us with a source of income, but it also delivers to us a great deal of self-satisfaction.

—Nancy Pierce
Superintendent
The Links at Crowbush Cove, Morell,
Prince Edward Island

The difficult 219 yard, par 3,
8th hole at Crowbush Cove

The spectacular 9th and 10th at Pebble Beach

We are discovering that improved stewardship of environmental assets offers us a chance to increase our professional satisfaction, adds a new dimension to our jobs, improves understanding in our business and within our neighboring communities, and makes a positive contribution to the environment.

—Edward C. Horton
CGCS, Vice President, Resource Management
Pebble Beach Company

The golf course is a complex and managed ecosystem. The important environmental issues confronting the location, design, construction, and operation of golf courses include many of the scientific interests that shape modern ecosystem research. For example, ecological engineering and ecosystem restoration contribute concepts and methods for providing and protecting the valuable natural areas for the plants, birds, and other wildlife that inhabit the course. Ecosystem energetics reminds us that solar energy transformed by plants sustains the golf course and determines the quality of playing conditions. Timely additions of water and nutrients in proper amounts, based on scientific understanding, are essential for growth. Effective course management may in turn help us understand other ecosystems that are less amenable to manipulation or study. Risks of disrupting the ecological integrity of the golf course posed by pests and disease require scientifically based and adaptive management practices similar in complexity and sophistication to those used in managing renewable agroecosystems, forests, and fisheries. Ecologically sound management practices can ensure that golf courses serve as environmental assets, to be enjoyed and appreciated by golfers now and in the future.

> Ecologically sound management practices can ensure that golf courses serve as environmental assets

Golf began as a game strongly influenced by the ecology of the Scottish linksland. Today, intelligent siting, thoughtful design, and careful consideration can produce courses that are again ecologically integrated with the surrounding landscape, and perhaps revitalize the earlier spirit of golf. Even as the game teaches us much about ourselves, its fields of play can provide keen insights concerning the complex ecological relationships that characterize and sustain both managed and natural ecosystems.

—**Dr. Steven M. Bartell**
Vice President and Director
SENES Oak Ridge Inc.
Center for Risk Analysis

St. Andrews

I was practicing on the *machair*, hitting short irons into the 9th green, when I suddenly became aware of my solitude. With the warm sun at my back, I wandered over to the boundary fence and took in the surrounding crofts: the green meadows filled with grazing sheep, the stone cottages, the bare brown mountains beyond the main road.

Travelers to the Western Isles invariably remark on the luminosity of the light, the depth and texture of the colors. It's as if the landscape were made by an artist laying on translucent glazes with a knife. The sounds—lambs bleating, a whippoorwill's droll warble—seem similarly layered. The buzz of an insect catches the ear as surely as the sharp squeal of a sea bird.

In my golf clothes, I felt vaguely foolish. Odd, considering that golf had been played there for a century.

—John Garrity
Sports Illustrated

The 197 yard, par 3, 12th hole at Wilderness Valley's Black Forest Course, Gaylord, MI

Golf evolved from nature. And in golf lies the sustenance of nature. Golf courses provide the perfect sanctuary for the preservation and perpetuation of plant ecosystems which are rapidly disappearing from the developed world. Prairies, dunes, deserts, wetlands, mountains, links, trees, shrubs, grasses, and endangered species can all find a home on the golf course where they can be maintained, sustained, and preserved for future generations.

The environment determines what happens in golf; how the golfer reacts with nature and the environment, either overcoming or succumbing to the environmental elements presented at each hole. Golf is the environment. Golf doesn't control the environment; the environment controls golf. By providing different and unique settings for the game, golf is influenced by the environment that surrounds it and enhances that environment by allowing people to interact with nature in these settings. This is the true beauty of golf—it utilizes what nature provides for us and enhances it, giving new meaning to the world around us—and continuing to do so for future generations.

—**Mike DeVries**
Design Associate
Fazio Golf Course Design

The par 4, 10th hole at the Golf Club of Georgia, plays 446 yards

When I ask my turfgrass students why they chose the golf course management profession, they generally always reference the love of working outdoors, in the environment. By the time they become golf course superintendents they will have been inundated with environmental enhancement information and it will be only second nature to practice this, as I do today.

I am convinced environmental responsibility is strongly self-enforced in our profession and would look for that trend to remain. There is no greater environmentalist than today's golf course superintendent.

—**Randy J. Waldron**
Director of Golf Courses and Landscaping
The Golf Club of Georgia, Alpharetta, GA

The pretty, but dangerous gorse, at the Old Course at St. Andrews, site of 25 Open Championships

Charles Darwin unlocked the secrets of evolution and taught us about natural selection and survival of the fittest. A view from the rough allows a golfer to see how plant breeding and artificial selection have improved golf course playing surfaces—better lies, truer putts, darker greens, and better persistence while using less water and chemicals. A golf course should embrace what nature has provided and what humans have improved. The game of golf should lead the way toward harmony between humanity and nature.

—Dr. Michael P. Kenna
Director, Turfgrass Research
U.S. Golf Association-Green Section

As one component of their environmental management plan, Old Westbury Golf & Country Club has developed a composting plan. Club superintendent Phil Anderson initiated the program that utilizes organic debris generated on the site as well as through a cooperative program with the Village of Old Westbury. Through this mutually beneficial arrangement, the Village disposes of yard waste and the Course produces rich composted soil. By the spring of 1995, Anderson had composted between 8,000 and 10,000 yards of debris, of which 75 percent was generated by the Village.

The Gleneagles Hotel Estate is an excellent example of an ideal inland golfing ground. The golf course architect, James Braid, made excellent use of the ridge and valley landforms to produce elevated tees, plateau and basin greens, and sunken (isolated) fairways between the send and gravel ridges (eskers).

The vegetation of this estate prior to human modification (i.e., at least five thousand years ago) would have been a mixed forest consisting mainly of oak, birch, and pine. Centuries of land management have produced a much more open vegetation cover with some mature trees plus broom (whin), heather, and the golf course grasses.

The 15th hole consists of an elevated tee with the fairway winding between 30 foot high ridges of sand and gravel. All of the topographical features are natural and required no earth movement.

—Dr. Robert J. Price

The 15th hole on the King's Course at
Gleneagles, Scotland

The 17th at Double Eagle Club, Galena, OH, 302 yards, dual fairway, drivable par 4

I love working on a golf course, not only for the smell of freshly mowed grass, but for the pleasure of watching golfers relaxing, enhancing their psyche and physical health; listening to the sound of birds and their pleasant voices; witnessing the beauty of golf turfgrasses, native grasses, and wildflowers seemingly everpresent forever underneath the trees blowing back and forth in the wind; having the course maintained in beautiful condition all season long for the sport of it and seeing many forms of wildlife in their natural state just being themselves.

Somehow, this all seems very right and the crowded sprawls of asphalt, concrete, and urban blight seem, oh, so very wrong.

—**Terry Buchen**
CGCS, Master Greenkeeper, Superintendent
Double Eagle Club

Kauai Lagoons Resort, Lihue, HI

The treacherous par 4, 5th hole at Oakmont.

I never imagined that I'd come to the city and see the wildlife that I see, day in and day out, at Oakmont. My first day on the job I saw a flock of wild turkeys and deer, and have since sighted red and grey fox, great-horned owls, hawks, Baltimore orioles, and countless other birds. In one newly established native area on the course there were over 100 goldfinch feeding on the seedhead. In addition to the course itself, Oakmont has over 200 acres of natural forest and native areas that make ideal habitat for all wildlife.

—**Mark Kuhns**
CGCS, Superintendent
Oakmont Country Club, Oakmont, PA

Through most of golf's centuries-old history, golf course management really wasn't a profession. It was basically greenkeeping: mowing, fertilizing, watering, cultivating, and so on. I'm not trying to deny the challenge of greenkeeping. It was, is and always will be challenging. Today, however, "greenkeeping" is only one element of golf course management. Today, a golf course superintendent is responsible for the care, maintenance, and improvement of what is often a multimillion-dollar property.

This business management role requires a great deal of professionalism. The golf course itself represents a technically complex, long-term capital investment in the form of a living ecosystem. The golf course superintendent is the individual responsible for every facet of its day-to-day and long-term management. In fulfilling this responsibility, the golf course superintendent synthesizes agronomic expertise and good environmental stewardship with business acumen, problem-solving abilities, and leadership and communication skills.

—**Bruce R. Williams**
CGCS, Vice President
Golf Course Superintendents Association of America

*The perilous 406 yard, par 4,
15th hole at Pelican Hill Golf Club,
Ocean Course, Newport Coast, CA.*

Designing and building a golf course in an environment like Mauna Lani requires a sensitive hand. The lava rock, although a very hard substance, is quite fragile on the surface. If care was not taken, the beauty would be lost forever. It was critical to apply all of our experience, imagination, and knowledge to preserve this special piece of earth while making its spectacular beauty accessible through the creation of the golf course. The stark contrast of the black *a'a* lava, the clear blue Pacific Ocean, the white sand, and the swaying palm trees, both captures the soul and triggers the adrenalin.

—**Robin Nelson**
Nelson • Wright • Haworth

Mauna Lani Resort, Kohala Coast, HI

The moderate length, par 4, 16th at the Plantation Course on Kapalua Resort plays through the strong trade winds crossing from the players left.

Spectacular tree specimens, seldom-seen birds, bodies of water full of life, amazing landscape views—this is what I experience in a golf course, not to mention the enjoyment of the game itself. Golf courses are flora and fauna oases. They are one of the best examples of coexistence I can think of.

Few people understand the management skills required to maintain a golf course, to maintain that high level of coexistence. Lawn mowers, fertilizers, pesticides, constant human intervention; yet, beautiful flora and fauna. How come? The professional golf course superintendent, integrated pest management, agronomy, personnel management and training.

Diagnostic tools, control programs, and pesticides are all part of Integrated Pest Management programs. These programs are very good examples of the industry getting together and developing pest control solutions to satisfy the needs of the golf player, the community, and the environment.

—Jose Milan
Ciba Turf and Ornamental Products

The Gleneagles Golf Course at Equinox, Manchester Village, VT

The nation's golf courses are a national treasure. They are aesthetically appealing, provide for health recreation and are a major habitat for wildlife in urban areas. Golf courses and other green spaces within a community are an economic asset. Additionally, they filter airborne pollutants and purify the water that filters through plant systems into the ground water.

Golf courses are ideal for disposal and utilization of nonpotable/recycled or waste waters. The dense sward slows runoff water and the extensive fibrous root system utilizes and filters impurities. Because of these processes, fertilizer and chemicals, when applied in accordance with recommendations, make the golf course environmentally safe.

—Dr. James R. Watson
Vice President, Agronomist
The Toro Company

Cabo del Sol, Cabo San Lucas, Mexico

The sun sets on the 12th hole at the Ocean Course at Kiawah Island.

The Ocean Course, located on the eastern tip of Kiawah Island, SC, is best known for its accolades during the 29th Ryder Cup. Its presence captured the world of golf, and it became the most talked about venue in the history of the event. Never before has a golf course received such worldwide attention. Pete Dye put it in perspective when he said, "No other course in the Northern Hemisphere has as many seaside holes." With natural dunes of sand and spacious wetlands, the Ocean Course takes into account the most natural elements Mother Nature has to offer. Its intimidating carries from tee to green, and the ocean sunset are a spectacular setting for both golf and nature. As the Ocean Course looks over the sea of waves, we are faced with the ultimate challenge of preserving golf and the environment together. With an ever-changing ecosystem, the evolution of this great golf course is constantly in touch with the demands and disciplines that make it special. Whether it is a Brown Pelican gliding along an open marsh, or a golfer carving his way out of a dune-shaped bunker, life on the Ocean Course is full of calm, excitement, and adventure.

—George L. Frye, Jr.
Superintendent
Ocean Course at Kiawah Island, SC

During the 1991 Ryder Cup, the 17th hole humbled some of the finest players in the world

Green grass is not an indictment of some sort of pollution. Unfortunately, many people consider the presence of well-maintained turf as an excessive use of inputs like fertilizer and pesticides, and that it will adversely impact our environmental resources. Research, however, indicates that the turfgrass ecosystem is a dynamic system that can efficiently process inputs, and the potential for impact from these products is inconsequential when managed properly. In addition, a turfgrass stand can offer protection to surface and ground water by controlling soil erosion and filtering water as it moves across the surface or downward in the soil profile.

> Green grass is not an indictment of some sort of pollution.

Golf course superintendents have a challenging, yet exciting profession. Their overlying charge is to provide an enjoyable playing surface. Their privilege is to feature the course in concert with the natural features of the property.

—**Dr. Gregory T. Lyman**
Michigan State University
Turfgrass Environmental Education Program

A home for wildlife, Cypress Point

The 17th at Medinah

At Medinah, which is located 10 miles from O'Hare International Airport, we have over 650 acres of green space and more than 10,000 mature trees tended by a full-time arborist. We are a proud member of the Audubon Cooperative Sanctuary Program for Golf Courses.

—Daniel H. Quast
CGCS, Grounds Manager
Medinah Country Club, Medinah, IL

The native fescues at Indianwood provide unique and challenging playing conditions, natural wildlife habitat, reduced maintenance costs, and scenic beauty that would make the player think that we are located in the British Isles.

—**Steven J. Hammon**
Old Course Superintendent
Indianwood Golf & Country Club, Lake Orion, MI

A golf course should lay lightly on the land, drawing both strategy and visual quality from the characteristics each site has to offer. An intimate relationship can be established with terrain and natural features through the design of a course, so that it will blend into the surrounding environment in a compatible and responsible manner. There are many sites however, that will have limited features on which a design can be based, due to their location or former use. In these instances, a golf course presents the opportunity to enhance the existing conditions on a site by creating conservation areas, promoting wildlife habitat, and preserving open space. As a result, the course can provide environmental benefits, in addition to recreational activity.

—William Love
Chair
Environmental Committee
American Society of Golf Course Architects

Olympia Fields Country Club, Olympia Fields, IL, site of the 1997 U.S. Senior Open Championship

Clearly, golf course superintendents must be motivated more by internal forces than by external praise—although they all deserve (and would probably welcome) more praise than they receive. What I hear, over and over, when I talk to superintendents is how much they love the land, as well as the things that grow and live on it.

—Joseph A. O'Brien
Chief Operating Officer
Golf Course Superintendents Association of
America

The 17th at Collier's Reserve—151 yards of native grasses and great golf.

Highly qualified, professional superintendents are masters of the art and science of golf course management. The superintendent interprets and uses scientific data and principles to improve the golf course and the environment. At the same time, the superintendent must understand the beauty of the game and the nuances of the golf course. The interplay of this art and science is geared to optimizing turf quality and enhancing the playing experience—within the framework of a fragile environment.

—David M. Bishop
Technical Information Services Manager
Golf Course Superintendents Association of America

According to a 1994 survey, more than 80 percent of golf course superintendents practice Integrated Pest Management (IPM).

Bear Creek Golf Club, Denver, CO

TPC of Michigan, site of the Ford Senior Players Championship

TPC of Michigan was built on 168 acres of reclaimed disturbed land within the urban setting of Detroit. On the course, 33 acres were restored to wetlands, native grasses, and shrubs in cooperation with the Michigan Department of Natural Resources. This is a brilliant example of business, government, and golf working together to create a better environment for golf and wildlife.

—Mike Giuffre
Superintendent
TPC of Michigan, Dearborn, MI

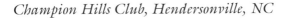
Champion Hills Club, Hendersonville, NC

Golf course architects have repeatedly designed golf courses and their communities around sensitive wetlands and upland habitat, but there is no single formula for success. Each project must be carefully studied and analyzed before work can begin.

Architects work diligently to protect and enhance the spectacular native beauty of a site. Special preservation techniques are developed for each project. The result: well-designed golf communities that both preserve the environmental integrity of the site and provide recreational opportunities for generations to come.

—Paul Fullmer
Executive Secretary
American Society of Golf Course Architects

Collier's Reserve, Naples, FL

The Ocean Course at Kiawah Island

One cannot emphasize too frequently the importance of leaving God's gifts alone and never fertilizing unless it is certain that time and nature will fail to cure.

—Dr. Alister MacKenzie
Golf Course Architect
(1870-1934)

One of the most significant changes in golf course management in the last 30 years is the dramatically increased interest in environmental matters, education and professionalism. While in the past fertilizers and chemicals may have been routinely applied, today's superintendent uses careful observation, integrated pest management, computers, and a more knowledgeable staff to more specifically control chemical applications. The modern superintendent is a true environmentalist who manages the course so that it supports the surrounding ecosystem.

—**Dr. Paul Rieke**
Michigan State University

May 3, 1995

Dear Collier's Reserve,

This was the best field trip I have ever been on. I had a magnificent time learning about conserving water, and you have done a marvelous job with preserving animals as well as trees. Your golf course is very neat and clean. The habitat that you have made for all kinds of animals is absolutely breathtaking. Thank you so much for having us. I will remember this trip forever.

Sincerely,
Whitney Bolyea

The 18th hole at Spring Island Golf Club, Callawassie, SC

Our environment is not only a guiding and governing aspect in golf course design, it is the tantamount element, when used properly, in achieving beauty, challenge, and variety.

Everyone who plays golf and who participates in golf course design is constantly looking for the course or the site that is beautiful, unusual, spectacular, and ever changing. All of these ingredients are found somewhere in our environment. Building golf courses in harmony with these environments gives everyone a better quality of life and a greater golfing experience.

—**Ed Seay**
Director of Design
Palmer Course Design Company

Golf courses are a gift to nature. An architect's job is to take the ground and improve on it, including the water, the soil, and the wildlife habitat.

—**Gary Player**
Gary Player Design Company

Royal Lytham & St. Annes, site of one of Gary Player's most emphatic victories in the 1974 Open Championship

Cobblestone Country Club, Stuart, FL

Most of us live in the urban world. Unfortunately, our city environments are all too often characterized by polluted air, crowded and congested streets, and a lack of flowing streams and open landscape. Golf courses, if properly sited, designed, and managed, can be urban reservoirs of wildlife habitat, vegetation, and urban green space.

When planned with these broader objectives in mind, golf courses provide significant benefits to a wide variety of wildlife and to the nongolfing public.

—**Paul Parker**
Center for Resource Management

PHOTOGRAPHIC CREDITS
(Photographer by page number)

David Bailey: i., v., 20, 34, 120, 130
William C. Minarich Photography: vi (as appeared on the cover of
    January 1995 *Golf Course Management*)
Wes Gray: vii
Mark Brown/Golf Stock: 4(Atlantic), 10, 12-13, 58, 132
Kent Davidson: 4(Industry), 14
Lindsay Ervin: 15
Mark Lucas: 22, 43, 81
Catherine Waterhouse: 27, 85
Steve Beeman: 28, 60
Philip Bailey: 30
Ron Smith: 38
Marcia Juergens: 40
David Fearis: 45
Greg Williams: 52, 53
Nancy Pierce: 54, 102
Teri Yamada: 55
Chris John/PDI: 57(Ervin)
Jane McAlonan: 57(Duck)
Tom Doak: 73, 98, 104, 105
Len Zorif: 78(panorama)
Old Westbury Golf & Country Club: 78(compost)
John Anderson: 83 (Oregon Golf Club)
Kristen Finnegan Photography: 83(owl)
Loch Lomond Golf Club: 86(pheasant)
Mike Hurdzan: 88
Mike DeVries: 92, 106
Garland Resort: 94, 95
P. Stan George: 96, 97
Jerry Coldiron: 100
Terry Buchen 110
Curt Norman: 119
Indianwood Golf & Country Club: 122
Mike Giuffre: 126
George Frye: 129

Excerpt p.105 reprinted courtesy of *Sports Illustrated.*

ACKNOWLEDGMENT

A View from the Rough is the work of many people. A special thanks to those representing the golf courses who assisted in preparation of this book. I must also thank the golf course superintendents, golf course architects and environmental professionals. Their insight and wisdom is clearly evident, and I hope that golfers may learn from them.